THIS JOURNAL

Belongs To:

_____

Start Date: _____

End Date: _____

One-Minute Daily Gratitude Journal

Life can be an emotional roller coaster, with times of ups and downs. When you're feeling down, it may seem easier to give in or ignore the problem; however, taking a moment to remind yourself of what is good around you by keeping a daily gratitude journal has been proven effective at helping people keep perspective when life throws them curveballs. A few moments each day dedicated to recognizing the good things will go far in terms of creating positive change both externally and internally!

Numerous scientific studies have found that gratitude has many emotional and mental benefits! Keeping a gratitude journal helps deal with difficult emotions and improves relationships. Showing appreciation helps us feel better connected to those we care about most.

This journal could be the key that unlocks profound transformation in your life. Taking just one minute each day to focus on all the good things around you, including the little ones, can make vast differences in your happiness and well-being. Happy gratitude journaling!

HOW TO USE THIS JOURNAL

To make gratitude journaling a habit and reap its benefits, set aside one minute each day to reflect on what you are grateful for that day. Keeping it simple and focusing on the basics can help avoid getting overwhelmed and keep the practice sustainable. Here's a summary of how to use this journal:

A. Set aside one minute each day to reflect on what you are grateful for.
B. Keep it simple and focus on the basics.
C. Be consistent and make it a daily habit.
D. Make note of missed opportunities to thank someone.

By using this format, you can create a one-minute gratitude journal that helps you focus on the good things in your life, seize opportunities to express gratitude towards others, and cultivate a positive mindset. This can help you develop a sense of appreciation towards those who make a positive impact on your life, even during a busy day. Perhaps more importantly, do not forget to be grateful for yourself. Afterall, you took the initiative to start this gratitude journal.

The One-Minute Daily Journal Overview

Each page is organized by the following categories:

• *Date*

• *List two to three things you are thankful for today.*

Examples are:
- Personal blessings (e.g., health, home, job).
- Interpersonal blessings (e.g., family, friends, significant other).
- Other blessings (e.g., opportunities, experiences, hobbies).

• *List of missed opportunities to thank someone.*
- Name specific individuals who have had a positive impact on your life.
- Briefly describe why you are grateful for them and how they have made a difference.
- Reflect on missed opportunities to express your gratitude towards them.

CONCLUSION

Cultivating gratitude through journaling is a practice that is simple yet powerful, offering significant benefits to everyone. Given the unique challenges and pressures we all face, taking time each day to focus on the positive and express gratitude can incredibly impact our mental and physical well-being.

There are four key takeaways from this discussion:

1. People tend to focus on others' needs and neglect their own emotional and psychological well-being, which can lead to stress-related illnesses.

2. Societal pressures and expectations related to appearance, relationships, and caregiving can increase stress levels and negatively affect mental health.

3. Gratitude journaling can help shift focus toward positive aspects of life and cultivate a more optimistic outlook, increasing feelings of happiness, contentment, and overall well-being.

4. Research has shown that keeping a daily gratitude journal can also have physical health benefits, such as improved sleep and reduced symptoms of stress and depression.

Therefore, we must prioritize well-being by incorporating gratitude journaling into our daily routines. By reflecting on the positive aspects of our lives, individuals can develop a stronger sense of self and increased self-esteem, which can help us better navigate societal pressures and expectations. So, let's make gratitude journaling a daily habit and reap the benefits for our mental and physical health.

One-Minute Daily Gratitude

Date: _____

List 2 to 3 things that you are thankful for today:

_____

_____

_____

List of missed opportunities to thank someone:

_____

_____

_____

Notes:

_____

_____

_____

_____

_____

One-Minute Daily Gratitude

Date: _____

List 2 to 3 things that you are thankful for today:

_____

_____

_____

List of missed opportunities to thank someone:

_____

_____

_____

Notes:

_____

_____

_____

_____

_____

One-Minute Daily Gratitude

Date: _____

List 2 to 3 things that you are thankful for today:

_____

_____

_____

List of missed opportunities to thank someone:

_____

_____

_____

Notes:

_____

_____

_____

_____

_____

One-Minute Daily Gratitude

Date: _____

List 2 to 3 things that you are thankful for today:

_____

_____

_____

List of missed opportunities to thank someone:

_____

_____

_____

Notes:

_____

_____

_____

_____

_____

One-Minute Daily Gratitude

Date: _____

List 2 to 3 things that you are thankful for today:

_____

_____

_____

List of missed opportunities to thank someone:

_____

_____

_____

Notes:

_____

_____

_____

_____

_____

One-Minute Daily Gratitude

Date: _____

List 2 to 3 things that you are thankful for today:

_____

_____

_____

List of missed opportunities to thank someone:

_____

_____

_____

Notes:

_____

_____

_____

_____

_____

One-Minute Daily Gratitude

Date: _____

List 2 to 3 things that you are thankful for today:

_____

_____

_____

List of missed opportunities to thank someone:

_____

_____

_____

Notes:

_____

_____

_____

_____

_____

One-Minute Daily Gratitude

Date: _____

List 2 to 3 things that you are thankful for today:

_____

_____

_____

List of missed opportunities to thank someone:

_____

_____

_____

Notes:

_____

_____

_____

_____

_____

One-Minute Daily Gratitude

Date: _____

List 2 to 3 things that you are thankful for today:

_____
_____
_____

List of missed opportunities to thank someone:

_____
_____
_____

Notes:

_____
_____
_____
_____

One-Minute Daily Gratitude

Date: _____

List 2 to 3 things that you are thankful for today:

_____

_____

_____

List of missed opportunities to thank someone:

_____

_____

_____

Notes:

_____

_____

_____

_____

_____

One-Minute Daily Gratitude

Date: _____

List 2 to 3 things that you are thankful for today:

_____
_____
_____

List of missed opportunities to thank someone:

_____
_____
_____

Notes:

_____
_____
_____
_____
_____

One-Minute Daily Gratitude

Date: _____

List 2 to 3 things that you are thankful for today:

_____

_____

_____

List of missed opportunities to thank someone:

_____

_____

_____

Notes:

_____

_____

_____

_____

_____

One-Minute Daily Gratitude

Date: _____

List 2 to 3 things that you are thankful for today:

_____

_____

_____

List of missed opportunities to thank someone:

_____

_____

_____

Notes:

_____

_____

_____

_____

_____

One-Minute Daily Gratitude

Date: _____

List 2 to 3 things that you are thankful for today:

_____

_____

_____

List of missed opportunities to thank someone:

_____

_____

_____

Notes:

_____

_____

_____

_____

_____

Ong Namo Guru Dev Namo

ute
titude

for today:

omeone:

Notes:

One-Minute Daily Gratitude

Date: _____

List 2 to 3 things that you are thankful for today:

_____

_____

_____

List of missed opportunities to thank someone:

_____

_____

_____

Notes:

_____

_____

_____

_____

_____

One-Minute Daily Gratitude

Date: _____

List 2 to 3 things that you are thankful for today:

_____

_____

_____

List of missed opportunities to thank someone:

_____

_____

_____

Notes:

_____

_____

_____

_____

_____

One-Minute Daily Gratitude

Date: _____

List 2 to 3 things that you are thankful for today:

_____
_____
_____

List of missed opportunities to thank someone:

_____
_____
_____

Notes:

_____
_____
_____
_____
_____

One-Minute Daily Gratitude

Date: _____

List 2 to 3 things that you are thankful for today:

_____
_____
_____

List of missed opportunities to thank someone:

_____
_____
_____

Notes:

_____
_____
_____
_____
_____

One-Minute Daily Gratitude

Date: _____

List 2 to 3 things that you are thankful for today:

_____

_____

_____

List of missed opportunities to thank someone:

_____

_____

_____

Notes:

_____

_____

_____

_____

_____

One-Minute Daily Gratitude

Date: _____

List 2 to 3 things that you are thankful for today:

_____

_____

_____

List of missed opportunities to thank someone:

_____

_____

_____

Notes:

_____

_____

_____

_____

One-Minute Daily Gratitude

Date: _____

List 2 to 3 things that you are thankful for today:

_____
_____
_____

List of missed opportunities to thank someone:

_____
_____
_____

Notes:

_____
_____
_____
_____
_____

One-Minute Daily Gratitude

Date: _____

List 2 to 3 things that you are thankful for today:

_____

_____

_____

List of missed opportunities to thank someone:

_____

_____

_____

Notes:

_____

_____

_____

_____

One-Minute Daily Gratitude

Date: _____

List 2 to 3 things that you are thankful for today:

_____

_____

_____

List of missed opportunities to thank someone:

_____

_____

_____

Notes:

_____

_____

_____

_____

_____

One-Minute Daily Gratitude

Date: _____

List 2 to 3 things that you are thankful for today:

_____

_____

_____

List of missed opportunities to thank someone:

_____

_____

_____

Notes:

_____

_____

_____

_____

One-Minute Daily Gratitude

Date: _____

List 2 to 3 things that you are thankful for today:

_____

_____

_____

List of missed opportunities to thank someone:

_____

_____

_____

Notes:

_____

_____

_____

_____

_____

One-Minute Daily Gratitude

Date: _____

List 2 to 3 things that you are thankful for today:

_____

_____

_____

List of missed opportunities to thank someone:

_____

_____

_____

Notes:

_____

_____

_____

_____

_____

One-Minute Daily Gratitude

Date: _____

List 2 to 3 things that you are thankful for today:

_____

_____

_____

List of missed opportunities to thank someone:

_____

_____

_____

Notes:

_____

_____

_____

_____

_____

One-Minute Daily Gratitude

Date: _____

List 2 to 3 things that you are thankful for today:

_____
_____
_____

List of missed opportunities to thank someone:

_____
_____
_____

Notes:

_____
_____
_____
_____
_____

One-Minute Daily Gratitude

Date: _____

List 2 to 3 things that you are thankful for today:

_____

_____

_____

List of missed opportunities to thank someone:

_____

_____

_____

Notes:

_____

_____

_____

_____

_____

One-Minute Daily Gratitude

Date: _____

List 2 to 3 things that you are thankful for today:

_____

_____

_____

List of missed opportunities to thank someone:

_____

_____

_____

Notes:

_____

_____

_____

_____

_____

One-Minute Daily Gratitude

Date: _____

List 2 to 3 things that you are thankful for today:

_____

_____

_____

List of missed opportunities to thank someone:

_____

_____

_____

Notes:

_____

_____

_____

_____

_____

One-Minute Daily Gratitude

Date: _____

List 2 to 3 things that you are thankful for today:

_____

_____

_____

List of missed opportunities to thank someone:

_____

_____

_____

Notes:

_____

_____

_____

_____

_____

One-Minute Daily Gratitude

Date: _____

List 2 to 3 things that you are thankful for today:

_____

_____

_____

List of missed opportunities to thank someone:

_____

_____

_____

Notes:

_____

_____

_____

_____

One-Minute Daily Gratitude

Date: _____

List 2 to 3 things that you are thankful for today:

_____

_____

_____

List of missed opportunities to thank someone:

_____

_____

_____

Notes:

_____

_____

_____

_____

One-Minute Daily Gratitude

Date: _____

List 2 to 3 things that you are thankful for today:

_____

_____

_____

List of missed opportunities to thank someone:

_____

_____

_____

Notes:

_____

_____

_____

_____

_____

One-Minute Daily Gratitude

Date: _____

List 2 to 3 things that you are thankful for today:

_____

_____

_____

List of missed opportunities to thank someone:

_____

_____

_____

Notes:

_____

_____

_____

_____

_____

One-Minute Daily Gratitude

Date: _____

List 2 to 3 things that you are thankful for today:

_____
_____
_____

List of missed opportunities to thank someone:

_____
_____
_____

Notes:

_____
_____
_____
_____
_____

One-Minute Daily Gratitude

Date: _____

List 2 to 3 things that you are thankful for today:

_____

_____

_____

List of missed opportunities to thank someone:

_____

_____

_____

Notes:

_____

_____

_____

_____

_____

One-Minute Daily Gratitude

Date: _____

List 2 to 3 things that you are thankful for today:

_____

_____

_____

List of missed opportunities to thank someone:

_____

_____

_____

Notes:

_____

_____

_____

_____

_____

One-Minute Daily Gratitude

Date: _____

List 2 to 3 things that you are thankful for today:

_____

_____

_____

List of missed opportunities to thank someone:

_____

_____

_____

Notes:

_____

_____

_____

_____

_____

One-Minute Daily Gratitude

Date: _____

List 2 to 3 things that you are thankful for today:

_____

_____

_____

List of missed opportunities to thank someone:

_____

_____

_____

Notes:

_____

_____

_____

_____

_____

One-Minute Daily Gratitude

Date: _____

List 2 to 3 things that you are thankful for today:

_____

_____

_____

List of missed opportunities to thank someone:

_____

_____

_____

Notes:

_____

_____

_____

_____

_____

One-Minute Daily Gratitude

Date: _____

List 2 to 3 things that you are thankful for today:

_____

_____

_____

List of missed opportunities to thank someone:

_____

_____

_____

Notes:

_____

_____

_____

_____

_____

One-Minute Daily Gratitude

Date: _____

List 2 to 3 things that you are thankful for today:

_____
_____
_____

List of missed opportunities to thank someone:

_____
_____
_____

Notes:

_____
_____
_____
_____

One-Minute Daily Gratitude

Date: _____

List 2 to 3 things that you are thankful for today:

_____
_____
_____

List of missed opportunities to thank someone:

_____
_____
_____

Notes:

_____
_____
_____
_____
_____

One-Minute Daily Gratitude

Date: _____

List 2 to 3 things that you are thankful for today:

_____

_____

_____

List of missed opportunities to thank someone:

_____

_____

_____

Notes:

_____

_____

_____

_____

_____

One-Minute Daily Gratitude

Date: _____

List 2 to 3 things that you are thankful for today:

_____

_____

_____

List of missed opportunities to thank someone:

_____

_____

_____

Notes:

_____

_____

_____

_____

_____

One-Minute Daily Gratitude

Date: _____

List 2 to 3 things that you are thankful for today:

_____
_____
_____

List of missed opportunities to thank someone:

_____
_____
_____

Notes:

_____
_____
_____
_____
_____

One-Minute Daily Gratitude

Date: _____

List 2 to 3 things that you are thankful for today:

_____

_____

_____

List of missed opportunities to thank someone:

_____

_____

_____

Notes:

_____

_____

_____

_____

_____

One-Minute Daily Gratitude

Date: _____

List 2 to 3 things that you are thankful for today:

_____

_____

_____

List of missed opportunities to thank someone:

_____

_____

_____

Notes:

_____

_____

_____

_____

One-Minute Daily Gratitude

Date: _____

List 2 to 3 things that you are thankful for today:

_____
_____
_____

List of missed opportunities to thank someone:

_____
_____
_____

Notes:

_____
_____
_____
_____
_____

One-Minute Daily Gratitude

Date: _____

List 2 to 3 things that you are thankful for today:

_____

_____

_____

List of missed opportunities to thank someone:

_____

_____

_____

Notes:

_____

_____

_____

_____

_____

One-Minute Daily Gratitude

Date: _____

List 2 to 3 things that you are thankful for today:

_____

_____

_____

List of missed opportunities to thank someone:

_____

_____

_____

Notes:

_____

_____

_____

_____

_____

One-Minute Daily Gratitude

Date: _____

List 2 to 3 things that you are thankful for today:

_____

_____

_____

List of missed opportunities to thank someone:

_____

_____

_____

Notes:

_____

_____

_____

_____

One-Minute Daily Gratitude

Date: _____

List 2 to 3 things that you are thankful for today:

_____

_____

_____

List of missed opportunities to thank someone:

_____

_____

_____

Notes:

_____

_____

_____

_____

_____

One-Minute Daily Gratitude

Date: _____

List 2 to 3 things that you are thankful for today:

_____

_____

_____

List of missed opportunities to thank someone:

_____

_____

_____

Notes:

_____

_____

_____

_____

One-Minute Daily Gratitude

Date: _____

List 2 to 3 things that you are thankful for today:

_____

_____

_____

List of missed opportunities to thank someone:

_____

_____

_____

Notes:

_____

_____

_____

_____

_____

One-Minute Daily Gratitude

Date: _____

List 2 to 3 things that you are thankful for today:

_____

_____

_____

List of missed opportunities to thank someone:

_____

_____

_____

Notes:

_____

_____

_____

_____

One-Minute Daily Gratitude

Date: _____

List 2 to 3 things that you are thankful for today:

_____

_____

_____

List of missed opportunities to thank someone:

_____

_____

_____

Notes:

_____

_____

_____

_____

_____

_____

One-Minute Daily Gratitude

Date: _____

List 2 to 3 things that you are thankful for today:

_____

_____

_____

List of missed opportunities to thank someone:

_____

_____

_____

Notes:

_____

_____

_____

_____

One-Minute Daily Gratitude

Date: _____

List 2 to 3 things that you are thankful for today:

_____
_____
_____

List of missed opportunities to thank someone:

_____
_____
_____

Notes:

_____
_____
_____
_____
_____

One-Minute Daily Gratitude

Date: _____

List 2 to 3 things that you are thankful for today:

_____

_____

_____

List of missed opportunities to thank someone:

_____

_____

_____

Notes:

_____

_____

_____

_____

One-Minute Daily Gratitude

Date: _____

List 2 to 3 things that you are thankful for today:

_____

_____

_____

List of missed opportunities to thank someone:

_____

_____

_____

Notes:

_____

_____

_____

_____

_____

One-Minute Daily Gratitude

Date: _____

List 2 to 3 things that you are thankful for today:

_____

_____

_____

List of missed opportunities to thank someone:

_____

_____

_____

Notes:

_____

_____

_____

_____

One-Minute Daily Gratitude

Date: _____

List 2 to 3 things that you are thankful for today:

_____

_____

_____

List of missed opportunities to thank someone:

_____

_____

_____

Notes:

_____

_____

_____

_____

_____

One-Minute Daily Gratitude

Date: _____

List 2 to 3 things that you are thankful for today:

_____
_____
_____

List of missed opportunities to thank someone:

_____
_____
_____

Notes:

_____
_____
_____
_____
_____

One-Minute Daily Gratitude

Date: _____

List 2 to 3 things that you are thankful for today:

_____
_____
_____

List of missed opportunities to thank someone:

_____
_____
_____

Notes:

_____
_____
_____
_____
_____

One-Minute Daily Gratitude

Date: _____

List 2 to 3 things that you are thankful for today:

_____

_____

_____

List of missed opportunities to thank someone:

_____

_____

_____

Notes:

_____

_____

_____

_____

One-Minute Daily Gratitude

Date: _____

List 2 to 3 things that you are thankful for today:

_____

_____

_____

List of missed opportunities to thank someone:

_____

_____

_____

Notes:

_____

_____

_____

_____

_____

One-Minute Daily Gratitude

Date: _____

List 2 to 3 things that you are thankful for today:

_____

_____

_____

List of missed opportunities to thank someone:

_____

_____

_____

Notes:

_____

_____

_____

_____

One-Minute Daily Gratitude

Date: _____

List 2 to 3 things that you are thankful for today:

_____

_____

_____

List of missed opportunities to thank someone:

_____

_____

_____

Notes:

_____

_____

_____

_____

_____

One-Minute Daily Gratitude

Date: _____

List 2 to 3 things that you are thankful for today:

_____

_____

_____

List of missed opportunities to thank someone:

_____

_____

_____

Notes:

_____

_____

_____

_____

_____

One-Minute Daily Gratitude

Date: _____

List 2 to 3 things that you are thankful for today:

_____
_____
_____

List of missed opportunities to thank someone:

_____
_____
_____

Notes:

_____
_____
_____
_____
_____

One-Minute Daily Gratitude

Date: _____

List 2 to 3 things that you are thankful for today:

_____

_____

_____

List of missed opportunities to thank someone:

_____

_____

_____

Notes:

_____

_____

_____

_____

_____

One-Minute Daily Gratitude

Date: _____

List 2 to 3 things that you are thankful for today:

_____

_____

_____

List of missed opportunities to thank someone:

_____

_____

_____

Notes:

_____

_____

_____

_____

_____

One-Minute Daily Gratitude

Date: _____

List 2 to 3 things that you are thankful for today:

_____

_____

_____

List of missed opportunities to thank someone:

_____

_____

_____

Notes:

_____

_____

_____

_____

One-Minute Daily Gratitude

Date: _____

List 2 to 3 things that you are thankful for today:

_____

_____

_____

List of missed opportunities to thank someone:

_____

_____

_____

Notes:

_____

_____

_____

_____

_____

One-Minute Daily Gratitude

Date: _____

List 2 to 3 things that you are thankful for today:

_____
_____
_____

List of missed opportunities to thank someone:

_____
_____
_____

Notes:

_____
_____
_____
_____

One-Minute Daily Gratitude

Date: _____

List 2 to 3 things that you are thankful for today:

_____
_____
_____

List of missed opportunities to thank someone:

_____
_____
_____

Notes:

_____
_____
_____
_____
_____

One-Minute Daily Gratitude

Date: _____

List 2 to 3 things that you are thankful for today:

_____

_____

_____

List of missed opportunities to thank someone:

_____

_____

_____

Notes:

_____

_____

_____

_____

_____

One-Minute Daily Gratitude

Date: _____

List 2 to 3 things that you are thankful for today:

_____

_____

_____

List of missed opportunities to thank someone:

_____

_____

_____

Notes:

_____

_____

_____

_____

_____

One-Minute Daily Gratitude

Date: _____

List 2 to 3 things that you are thankful for today:

_____

_____

_____

List of missed opportunities to thank someone:

_____

_____

_____

Notes:

_____

_____

_____

_____

_____

One-Minute Daily Gratitude

Date: _____

List 2 to 3 things that you are thankful for today:

_____

_____

_____

List of missed opportunities to thank someone:

_____

_____

_____

Notes:

_____

_____

_____

_____

_____

One-Minute Daily Gratitude

Date: _____

List 2 to 3 things that you are thankful for today:

_____

_____

_____

List of missed opportunities to thank someone:

_____

_____

_____

Notes:

_____

_____

_____

_____

_____

One-Minute Daily Gratitude

Date: _____

List 2 to 3 things that you are thankful for today:

_____
_____
_____

List of missed opportunities to thank someone:

_____
_____
_____

Notes:

_____
_____
_____
_____
_____

# One-Minute Daily Gratitude

Date: _____

List 2 to 3 things that you are thankful for today:

_____
_____
_____

List of missed opportunities to thank someone:

_____
_____
_____

Notes:

_____
_____
_____
_____

One-Minute Daily Gratitude

Date: _____

List 2 to 3 things that you are thankful for today:

_____

_____

_____

List of missed opportunities to thank someone:

_____

_____

_____

Notes:

_____

_____

_____

_____

_____

One-Minute Daily Gratitude

Date: _____

List 2 to 3 things that you are thankful for today:

_____

_____

_____

List of missed opportunities to thank someone:

_____

_____

_____

Notes:

_____

_____

_____

_____

_____

One-Minute Daily Gratitude

Date: _____

List 2 to 3 things that you are thankful for today:

_____

_____

_____

List of missed opportunities to thank someone:

_____

_____

_____

Notes:

_____

_____

_____

_____

_____

Notes

Date: _____

Notes

Date: _____

Notes

Date: _____

Notes

Date: _____

Notes

Date: _____

Notes

Date: _____